A group of continental scent bottles in various types of coloured glass including, from left, a bottle decorated with surface staining, two bottles painted with enamels and gilded, opaline bottles with gilded decoration and with silver-plated holder, cut-glass and cased-glass bottles. 1840-70.

SCENT BOTTLES

Alexandra Walker

Shire Publications Ltd

CONTENTS

Published in 1999 by Shire Publications Ltd, Cromwell House, Church Street, Princes Risborough, Buckinghamshire HP27 9AA, UK. Website: www.shirebooks.co.uk
Copyright © 1987 by Alexandra Walker. First published 1987; reprinted 1991, 1994, 1996 and 1999. Shire Album 210. ISBN 0 85263 909 0.

Printed in Great Britain by CIT Printing Services Ltd, Press Buildings, Merlins Bridge, Haverfordwest, Pembrokeshire SA61 1XF.

British Library Cataloguing in Publication Data: Walker, Alexandra. Scent bottles. — (Shire albums; 210). 1. Scent bottles — History. I. Title 748.8'2. NK5440.B6. ISBN 0-85263-909-0.

ACKNOWLEDGEMENTS
  I should like to thank all the museum curators, private owners and cosmetic companies who helped me in preparing this book. Particular thanks are due to Vivienne Bennett of the Harris Museum and Art Gallery, Preston, for allowing me to use so many illustrations of items from the Mrs C. A. L. French Bequest of over 2700 scent bottles. I should also like to thank Dr Edmund Launert for his advice and encouragement, and Barbara Conway and Anthony Hayes for help with photography. The cover illustration is by Norwyn Photographics of Preston.
  Photographs are acknowledged to: Birmingham Museum and Art Gallery, page 6; Bolton Museum and Art Gallery, page 5 (bottom right); Bonhams Ltd, page 28; Guerlain, page 32; Harris Museum and Art Gallery, Preston, pages 1, 2, 8 (right), 9, 13 (top, bottom right), 16, 17 (bottom), 18 (bottom), 19 (top), 20, 21, 22 (top, bottom right), 23, 24, 25, 27, 30; Liverpool Museum, National Museums and Galleries on Merseyside, pages 3, 4, 5 (top), 11; National Museum of Ireland, Dublin, page 13 (bottom left); Pilkington Glass Museum, page 5 (bottom left); Rimmel, page 15; Rotherham Museum and Beatson Clark, page 19 (bottom); The Royal Pavilion, Brighton, pages 26, 29; Science Museum, page 7; Sothebys, page 10; Spode Museum, pages 17 (top), 18 (top); Victoria and Albert Museum, pages 8 (left), 22 (bottom left); Ruth Warner Collection, page 31; Trustees of the Wedgwood Museum, Barlaston, page 12.

COVER: *A group of scent bottles from the Mrs C. A. L. French Bequest in the Harris Museum and Art Gallery, Preston. This remarkable collection of over 2700 bottles includes examples dating from the eighteenth to the early twentieth century in ceramics, glass and other materials.*

BELOW: *Silver-mounted cut-glass bottles. The two in the centre have tiny pierced pomanders which screw on to the caps. Two of the bottles have patch boxes in the sides. Some have engraved monograms under the foot and may have been used as seals. Dutch and English, late seventeenth century to early eighteenth century. Heights from 4 1/4 inches (108 mm) to 3 1/4 inches (83 mm).*

Alabaster and basalt scent bottles of the Egyptian Predynastic period (about 5000 to 3050 BC). Each has a lip to enable a covering to be tied on to the bottle. Heights 2 inches (50 mm) and 2⅜ inches (60 mm).

INTRODUCTION

The words perfume, from the Latin *per fumum* meaning 'by smoke', and incense, from *incendere* meaning 'to burn', remind us of the earliest uses of aromatic substances, burnt as part of religious ceremony. Incense burners have been found in Egyptian tombs, and wall paintings depict their use. Incense and the use of perfumes in ritual and civil ceremony were also an important element in the early Chinese culture, and incense has a long and continuing history of use in the Christian church.

Perfume has also been put to medicinal uses. Hippocrates wrote of the use of aromatic fumigation in preventing contagion, and later Arab doctors used perfumed substances to treat patients and also to scent their own garments. In England in the middle ages apothecaries used native herbs to make medicines. As trade with the east increased, these herbs were supplemented with exotic spices and aromatics such as cloves, cinnamon, sandalwood and frankincense. Substances with strong scents were believed to be protective against contagious diseases.

Pomanders were carried during the Great Plague of 1664-5. These could be oranges stuck with cloves or elaborate gold and silver boxes with compartments to hold a variety of aromatics.

Perfume is also valued for its ability to enhance the wearer's attractiveness. Who can say how old is human vanity? It seems that as soon as life has risen above the most basic struggle for existence some urge to care for the person and beautify the appearance asserts itself. Evidence of the use of cosmetics has been found in tombs of the Egyptian Predynastic period.

Scent has always been expensive to produce and its luxurious nature is reflected in the beauty of the containers made to hold it. Until the twentieth century it was usual for the customer to have her own bottle into which the scent she bought was decanted. Today the cosmetics and perfume industry is dominated by large multinational companies but, although some of the familiar names from the department stores first made their appearance as long ago as the end of

3

the eighteenth century, many perfumes were made by small local firms using ingredients such as otto of roses from Bulgaria, lavender from Provence, patchouli from India and ambergris from oceans. Books of recipes, like Septimus Piesse's *Art of Perfumery*, were published to enable chemists to make up their own stock of popular scents such as the Victorian bestselling *Jockey Club*. Today both the name of the scent and the design of the bottle in which it is sold are jealously protected from imitation.

THE EARLIEST SCENT BOTTLES

The earliest scent bottles were small stone jars and pottery vases used by the Egyptians to hold perfumed oils and unguents. Alabaster and basalt jars of the Predynastic period (about 5000 to 3050 BC) were hollowed out by drilling and have finely finished surfaces. Some have a narrow lip around the neck enabling a covering, possibly of leather, to be tied over the opening.

When glass was first made in Egypt in the Eighteenth Dynasty (1570 to 1293 BC) it was mostly used for scent and cosmetic bottles. Egyptian glass was not transparent and was admired for its resemblance to precious minerals. Small bottles were made by the core technique. An inner former of mud and straw was held on a metal rod and coated with a layer of molten glass. The bottles were typically made of dark blue opaque or translucent glass decorated with trailed stripes of yellow, white and pale blue glass which were combed with a sharp metal tool to form zigzag designs. The clay core was scraped out of the finished bottle when it had cooled.

Very many bottles made by this technique have been found in tombs and cemeteries in the Mediterranean area, traded by the Greeks from the sixth century BC. Perfume was an important element in Greek funeral rites at this time. Their shapes are miniature forms of the ceramics of the period. The Greeks also made scent bottles in terracotta, an unglazed earthenware. These include bottles in the form of animals, birds and human heads. Very fine bottles were made at Corinth about the sixth century BC. This was the centre which developed the famous 'black figure' painted ceramics, and scent bottles were decorated with lively paintings of birds, animals or human figures.

It was not until the technique of blowing glass was discovered about 50 BC in Syria, then part of the Roman empire, that the special qualities of glass could be exploited. Blown glass was translucent or even transparent and could be manipulated while in the semi-molten state. By blowing glass in a mould similar pieces could be made in quantity and so mass-production was possible. This method of making glass vessels rapidly spread throughout the Roman empire.

Moulded glass bottles in the form of a double-sided head, sometimes known as Janus flasks, were made in the second and third centuries AD. Blown glass can

Translucent blue glass bottle with combed trailed decoration in yellow and turquoise, made by the core technique. Egyptian, sixth to fifth century BC. Height 2½ inches (63 mm).

also be made in free forms, with the shaping being done by rolling the vessel on a smooth surface and by pincering it with metal tools. Many such bottles are made of colourless glass, decorated with applied threads of the same or coloured glass. This type of glass seems to have been made at several centres under Roman rule as far apart as Syria and Cologne.

LEFT: *Corinthian terracotta bottle of a shape known as an aryballos. Painted with a bird motif. 650-550 BC.*

BELOW LEFT: *Transparent green mould-blown flask in the form of a double-sided head. Roman, second or third century AD. Height 3⅛ inches (80 mm).*
BELOW RIGHT: *Colourless blown glass bottle with trailed bands around the neck and trailed handles of turquoise glass. Syrian, fourth century AD. Height 2¾ inches (71 mm).*

LEFT: *Silver-gilt scent bottle engraved with grotesques. The stopper is secured by tiny chains. English, about 1690. Height 1¾ inches (44 mm).*
RIGHT: *Mould-blown scent bottle of opaque blue glass splashed with white and yellow glass with flecked metallic inclusions, probably copper. Venetian, early eighteenth century. Height 3 inches (77 mm).*

SCENT CONTAINERS FROM THE MEDIEVAL TO STUART PERIODS

The use of perfume for personal enhancement went out of favour during the early Christian period, although incense continued to be used in religious ceremony. However, the Crusaders brought back a taste for luxurious perfumes from the Near East. By the end of the twelfth century perfumery was important enough to fall under the control of the guilds, and in the following centuries to be the subject of disputes between the Glovers, Haberdashers and Apothecaries. Perfume was used at the court of Henry VIII in several forms. Rooms were sprinkled with rosewater from 'casting bottles' and scented pastilles were burnt in 'fuming boxes'. For personal use 'sweet bags' filled with fragrant herbs were carried in the clothing or pomanders were hung on chains round the neck or from the waist.

Perfume was regarded as being useful in warding off infection. Pomanders (derived from *pomme*, meaning apple, which describes their shape, and *ambre*, or ambergris, which was one of the aromatics which they contained) were often made of precious metals and richly jewelled. Humbler examples were made of wood or earthenware. They were pierced to enable their owners to inhale the scent at will. They were widely used during the Great Plague of 1664-5 and a number of examples in silver and gold from this period are now in the Wellcome Museum of the History of Medicine, now part of the Science Museum. Some are made in segments, rather like an orange. Different herbs or aromatics would have been held in each compartment and pomanders are sometimes engraved with the names of the contents.

Silver and gold scent bottles from the second half of the seventeenth century are usually a flattened pear shape or baluster-shaped with a tapering neck. They are decorated with engraved scrollwork, grotesque or chinoiserie subjects and in some cases are enamelled. The stoppers are often secured by tiny chains.

During the middle ages Venice became

an important centre for glassmaking. As a great trading power with links with the Near East, Venice probably benefited from the influence of the Syrian glassmakers. Among the few scent-related items which survive from the early period of Venetian glassmaking are rosewater sprinklers in the Islamic style. Venice remained the most important glassmaking centre until the eighteenth century. In the sixteenth and seventeenth centuries highly decorative glass was made including the famous *latticino* glass which incorporated twisted opaque white canes in clear glass, multicoloured *millefiori* glass made up of coloured canes cut across the

A group of engraved silver pomanders. The separate segments contained aromatic herbs or wax-based perfumes which, it was believed, would help to ward off disease. English, seventeenth century.

grain, and glass incorporating tiny fragments of gold or copper to give a sparkling effect rather like the mineral aventurine.

In France opaque white and coloured glass scent bottles were among the products of Bernard Perrot's Orléans glasshouse, active during the second half of the seventeenth century. Pieces which are usually attributed to this factory include flattened pear-shaped moulded bottles with relief decoration incorporating motifs such as fleurs-de-lis, hearts and sunbursts. Bottles in the shape of human

heads may also originate from this factory.

By the late seventeenth century perfumes were valued more for their cosmetic than their medicinal properties. The art of the perfumer flourished, especially in France. The areas around Grasse and Montpellier became famous for the production of the flowers used in perfumery and remain important centres of the industry today. While the professional production of perfume expanded, it also became a fashionable amateur pursuit.

LEFT: *Mould-blown blue glass scent bottle with relief decoration of a crown and fleurs-de-lis. Made at the Orléans glassworks of Bernard Perrot. Late seventeenth century.*
RIGHT: *Mould-blown glass bottle in the shape of a negro's head, possibly made at the Orléans glassworks. Early eighteenth century. Height 2¼ inches (57 mm).*

A group of jasperware bottles, including an example of shape 1377 (right), which is shown in the Wedgwood factory shape-book. The centre bottle is a marked example by Turner. 1790-1820.

THE EIGHTEENTH CENTURY

In London signboards with emblems such as civet cats, roses and orange trees drew customers to the many new perfumers' shops which were opened during the eighteenth century. Perfumes could also be bought from jewellers and shops which sold 'toys', amusing trinkets which included enamel, glass and porcelain scent bottles.

Some of the most delightful rococo scent bottles of the mid eighteenth century were the painted enamels made at Bilston (West Midlands) and London. At first glance they look rather like porcelain but they are made of copper covered in an opaque white enamel glaze and painted. The decoration of these bottles includes all the frivolous subjects fashionable at the time: pastoral scenes with shepherds and shepherdesses, pretty young women, views of ruins and flowers. Scent bottles are sometimes combined with a bonbonnière, or box for sweets or cachous.

The bottles have gilt metal mounts,

often with stoppers in the shape of birds, which are usually attached to the bottle by a small chain. The making of metal mounts for snuffboxes, étuis, scent bottles and other 'toys' was a speciality of the area around Birmingham and Wolverhampton.

Contemporary with these enamels are opaque white and coloured glass scent and smelling bottles with painted and gilded decoration. They have chased silver or gold caps over ground-glass stoppers and were often supplied with shagreen cases. Many are believed to have been made in the Midlands, although opaque white and coloured glass was also made in Bristol and London. The London decorating studio of James Giles, best known for his work on porcelain, was probably responsible for a group decorated with gilded exotic birds and trees.

Colourless glass bottles with silver mounts were made in England and Holland. Bottles with silver boxes set into

ABOVE LEFT: *Enamel scent bottle painted with the profile of a young girl. The gilt metal scrolled stopper is secured by a chain. Bilston, about 1760. Height 4 inches (100 mm).*
ABOVE RIGHT: *Green glass scent bottle cut overall in shallow facets and decorated in coloured enamels and gilding with a riverside scene with fisherman. London or West Midlands, 1760-5. Height 2⅞ inches (73 mm).*
BELOW LEFT: *Chelsea porcelain double scent bottle in the form of a pair of billing doves. The gilt metal-mounted stoppers are modelled as moths and secured by fine chains. About 1760. Height 2¾ inches (70 mm).*
BELOW RIGHT: *Porcelain scent bottle from the 'Girl in a Swing' factory, in the form of a shepherdess with a lamb by her side. About 1749-54. Height 3⅜ inches (85 mm).*

their sides to hold patches or rouge remind us that cosmetics were used in lavish quantities by the fashionable. Dual-purpose bottles were also made with bases which could be used as seals, or with tiny pierced silver pomanders on the lids.

About 1743 a porcelain factory was established at Chelsea. Although scent bottles were not among the earliest products of the factory, they seem to have been very popular when they were introduced in the mid 1750s. They were often in the form of figures, sometimes with the head forming the stopper and the metal mount a collar round the neck. Others were shaped as fruit, birds or animals. Scent bottles were made at both the original Lawrence Street factory and at the short-lived breakaway 'Girl in a Swing' factory (named after a figure made by the company) believed to have been founded by Charles Gouyn, a partner of the original Chelsea company.

Scent bottles were included in the fitments of *nécessaires*, little caskets which held such items as mirrors, needlework and manicure tools and ivory writing tablets. They were made in enamel, porcelain and shagreen. A fine example in Liverpool Museum is fitted with glass bottles with tiny Chelsea porcelain stoppers.

Towards the end of the eighteenth century fashionable taste turned from the rococo to the more elegantly restrained neo-classicism. Josiah Wedgwood's jasperware perfectly suited the new style. This fine-grained unglazed stoneware with relief decoration in white on a coloured ground was introduced in 1775 and used for a wide variety of ornamental wares.

In 1788 Josiah Wedgwood wrote to his son mentioning scent bottles for the first time. 'The smelling bottles with the stadholder & the princess are very good & pretty things, particularly that with the festoon border of which pattern I would have the rest made . . . You need not make any stoppers to the bottles, they use cork ones!' There are frequent references to scent bottles in records dating from the 1790s. The factory shape-books illustrate examples decorated with classical subjects and portrait reliefs, such as

Shagreen nécessaire in the form of a miniature chest of drawers, containing four glass scent bottles, two of which have Chelsea porcelain bird-shaped stoppers. English, about 1755.

11

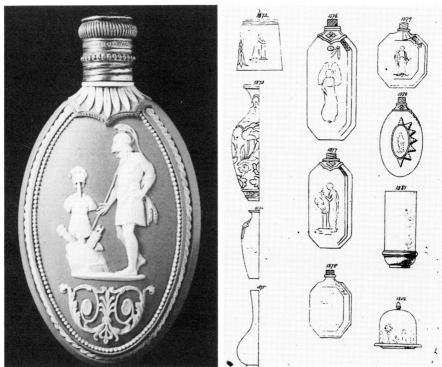

LEFT: *Jasperware scent bottle in the Wedgwood Museum, Barlaston. It shows 'Mars contemplating his armour' and is a fine example of a bottle in the neo-classical style. 1785-90. Height 3 inches (75 mm).*
RIGHT: *Detail of a page from the Wedgwood factory shape-book showing designs for scent bottles. About 1790-1800.*

those mentioned in Wedgwood's letter. They are shown with spirally threaded necks to take screw-on metal mounts.

Wedgwood's jasperware was copied by other potters including William Adams and John Turner, both of Staffordshire. A scent bottle in the Harris Museum and Art Gallery, Preston, has an impressed Turner mark, but the earliest Wedgwood bottles are unmarked.

At the end of the eighteenth century scent bottles were among the products of the Birmingham toymakers, manufacturers of small silver objects such as snuffboxes, vinaigrettes, shoe buckles and nutmeg graters. These took the form of silver bottles with screw tops, or silver cases with hinged lids which contained tiny glass bottles. These would have been easily obtainable from the many glassmakers working in the Midlands.

In the late eighteenth century there was a fashion for cut glass, a style of decoration ideally suited to English lead glass, though not at all to the Venetian soda glass. Glass cutters worked at a wheel, which in the eighteenth century was operated by foot, to grind away facets in the glass which when polished enhanced its sparkling brilliance. The rise in popularity of cut glass coincided with increased taxes which were levied on glass by weight. Ireland was free from these inhibiting levies and so glassmakers at Cork, Waterford, Dublin and Belfast were able to take advantage of their favourable position, making cut lead glass in the English style.

Two silver scent bottles by Cocks and Betteridge of Birmingham. Both have hallmarks for the year 1802. Heights (right) 1⅝ inches (42 mm) and (left) 2 inches (52 mm).

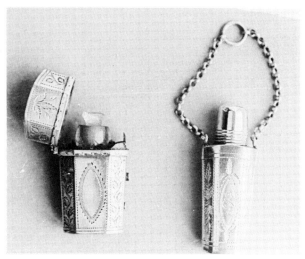

LEFT: *Cut-glass scent vial with the engraved inscription 'L' amitie vous l'offre Waterford Febry Th 15 1794'. In the National Museum of Ireland, Dublin. Length 5⅞ inches (150 mm).*
RIGHT: *Attar bottles in coloured and clear glass decorated with coloured enamels and gilding. Probably made in the Isergebirge region of Bohemia. Nineteenth century.*

13

Flat rectangular and shuttle-shaped scent vials were made at the end of the eighteenth century. An example in the National Museum of Ireland is dated 1794 in the engraved inscription. Larger cut-glass bottles were made in the first few decades of the nineteenth century. Typically they are squat in shape, with deeply cut pillar flutes and panels of diamond cutting.

A very different type of glass bottle which began to appear in the late eighteenth century was the attar bottle. These long narrow bottles are sometimes called 'throwaways' or, erroneously, 'Oxford lavenders'. In the opinion of Dr Edmund Launert they originate in the Iser Mountain region of Bohemia around the town of Jablonec. They are usually cut with shallow facets and decorated with coloured enamel designs which at their best have all the charm of a folk art but which can degenerate into crudeness. Attar of roses was sold in similar bottles until the early years of the twentieth century.

Two scent bottles showing the Irish style of cutting of the 1820s. The cut mushroom stoppers are typical of this period. Heights (right) 3⅝ inches (90 mm), (left) 2⅝ inches (73 mm).

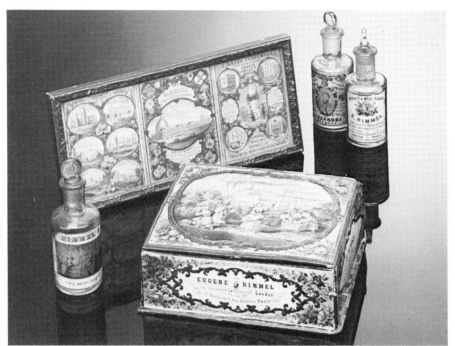

Eugene Rimmel perfumery of the 1860s. The bottle labels stress the firm's royal appointments, and two of the scents are named in honour of the Princess of Wales — 'The Alexandra Bouquet' and 'Royal Bridal Bouquet'.

THE NINETEENTH CENTURY

Scent bottles were made by many of the nineteenth-century, potteries. They were always a minor product but they reflect in miniature the styles and decorating techniques of their time. Wedgwood continued to make jasperware bottles in the nineteenth century and later also made bone-china bottles. The Derby and Spode factories both made elegant bottles with long narrow necks in the early nineteenth century. Coalport made a variety of bottles including examples with *pâte-sur-pâte* decoration which was painted in successive coats of white slip on a coloured ground, giving a slight relief effect. At the end of the century the Worcester Royal Porcelain Company made a series of shield-shaped bottles painted with flowers and birds. In the latter part of the nineteenth century quantities of inexpensive scent bottles were made in the Potteries.

The growth of tourism led to the manufacture of inexpensive souvenirs and many nineteenth-century bottles fall into this category. French opaline glass bottles have views printed on paper set into the lid, or into stamped metal cagework. German porcelain bottles have mottoes or the names of resorts painted among flowers. Some of these are mounted with crown-shaped stoppers which partially unscrew to form a sprinkler. Sparkling aventurine glass was used for souvenirs of Venice.

The collector of Victorian scent bottles is very likely to become interested in smelling-salt bottles and would probably find it hard to exclude them, for one of the most commonly found types is the double-ended bottle which holds perfume at one end and smelling salts at the other. The two ends can be distinguished by different types of lids. The scent bottle

ABOVE: *A pair of Derby porcelain scent bottles decorated in gold on a deep blue ground. Marked with a standard crowned 'D' painted mark. About 1815-25. Height 5 inches (126 mm).*
BELOW: *Royal Worcester bottles in white and ivory-coloured porcelain, hand-painted with flowers and birds. The example painted with irises is signed 'H. Everett'. 1890s. Height 4 inches (100 mm).*

Three scent bottles of a design described in the 1820 Spode shape-book as 'Lizard bottles', showing different styles of decoration. Height 4 inches (102 mm).

end usually has a screw top over a ground-glass stopper, while the smelling-salt end has a hinged lid with a spring-loaded fastener.

The Victorian lady, tightly laced into her corsets, must often have felt the need of a whiff of something bracing if one judges by the evidence of the numbers of smelling bottles which survive. The substances which were used fall into two main types and they affect the design of the container in which they were kept. Vinaigrettes had a pierced metal grille beneath the lid which held in place an absorbent material such as sponge or wool. This would be soaked with smelling

Souvenirs for the tourist including a Dutch earthenware bottle, a German bottle with sprinkler stopper, two French opaline glass bottles, and a group of Venetian glass bottles. Nineteenth century.

salts, which were basically liquid ammonia scented with rosemary, lavender, bergamot and cloves. Aromatic vinegars, based on acetic acid, were also used in the same way as liquid smelling salts and were believed to be beneficial in illness.

Smelling bottles with wide openings (which can be distinguished from scent bottles because the latter have narrow openings to protect the contents from spillage and evaporation) were used for salts in crystalline form. The cheapest type, Preston salts, was sold in bottles with the name moulded on the side, and these are sometimes found by bottle collectors in old rubbish dumps.

Eugene Rimmel was one of the most enterprising perfumers of the nineteenth century. His family was of French origin and owned flower farms in Grasse. Rimmel's father had been a pupil of the great Lubin, perfumer to the Empress Josephine, but moved to London to open a perfumery in Bond Street in the 1820s. Eugene Rimmel was a great publicist and at the Great Exhibition of 1851 he installed a giant Perfume Fountain and sold his *Great Exhibition Bouquet* in 'cut and stoppered bottles . . . ornamented with a view of the Crystal Palace'. Rimmel's publicity stunts included scenting the Lyceum Theatre with rose perfume for a performance of *Crystabelle or The Rose Without a Thorn*. His history of perfumery, *The Book of Perfumes*, was serialised in one of the leading women's magazines of the day and became a best seller translated into several languages.

During the nineteenth century some of the best-known companies including Guerlain and Rimmel began to sell scent in their own specially designed bottles.

ABOVE: *Spode scent bottle painted with sprays of flowers on a cobalt-blue ground with gilded stripes. Marked 'Spode' with the pattern number '2478'. Mid nineteenth century. Height 2⅛ inches (72 mm).*

RIGHT: *Double-ended bottles could hold scent at one end and smelling salts at the other. They usually have different types of stoppers at each end. 1870-90.*

Victorian smelling bottles. The wide-necked cased-glass bottle is for smelling-salt crystals. The other vinaigrettes of horn, agate and glass have pierced grilles. The cheaper examples have mass-produced stamped metal mounts; better examples have silver mounts. About 1865-85.

However, most perfumers still sold it in relatively plain bottles to be decanted into the buyer's own bottle. As perfume was used by more and more people glass manufacturers made scent bottles in a wide variety of styles and shapes.

The nineteenth century was a time of experimentation by glassmakers. New types of glass were introduced and new styles of decoration developed. The Bohemian glassmakers had a great influence on English manufacturers, particularly in the field of coloured glass. In the 1820s Friedrich Egermann invented 'lithyalin', an opaque reddish-brown coloured glass with veined marking rather like agate. This was particularly suited to massive shapes with broad flat planes which showed off the markings.

Coloured glass was extensively used for scent bottles. Some of the larger coloured glass toilet-water bottles of the 1830-50

Scent was sold in plain bottles, as shown here in a page from the catalogue of the Rotherham glassmakers Beatson and Clark. Shape 18 is described as the 'Oxford lavender' and was made in nine sizes ranging from 1/2 ounce (14 gram) to 8 ounce (227 gram) capacity. 1901.

period are more exuberantly than elegantly shaped. Bulbous bodies have flaring collars around the neck and scalloped feet, and they are topped with elaborately shaped stoppers, the whole being decorated with deep cutting.

Cased glass became very popular from the mid 1830s. This was a Bohemian invention but was soon copied by English glassmakers. Cased glass is made with layers of different colours in the body, which are revealed when the piece is cut.

Sometimes the glass is further embellished by enamelling and gilding, a feature of Bohemian glass in particular. Very many cased-glass scent bottles survive. Of several hundred bottles of this type in the Harris Museum and Art Gallery, Preston, the earliest datable example (from the hallmark on the silver mount) is from 1841 and the latest from the early years of the twentieth century.

The most influential English glassmaker of the nineteenth century was Apsley

An amusing French model of a horse-drawn cart laden with four scent bottles in white, red, blue and green opaline glass. Mid nineteenth century. Length 4½ inches (113 mm).

Pellatt (1791-1863). In 1819 he introduced a method of making *crystallo-ceramie,* glass with white ceramic cameos embedded in the metal. These are sometimes known as 'sulphides'. The cameos are usually profile portraits of notable personalities of his day. In 1831 he patented a method of making intaglio moulded glass. Scent bottles were made in both these types of glass, in combination with cutting. Scent bottles with cameo incrustations were also made in France.

The firm of Sampson Mordan, established about 1813, was one of the most prolific Victorian manufacturers of small personal possessions in silver and other metals. Among their products were pro-

Latticino decoration in white and colours is given a broken effect by the ribbed surface decoration which was achieved by mechanical threading or by blowing into a ribbed mould. The bottle on the left is probably St Louis. French, 1870s. Height of centre bottle 5¼ inches (132 mm).

21

Two bottles by Apsley Pellatt. One has a crystal-lo-ceramie cameo showing the profile busts of the four politicians (Grey, Brougham, Russell and Althorp) who championed the 1832 Reform Bill. Lord Grey is also portrayed in the intaglio decoration of the other bottle, which is marked PELLATT & C PATENTEES. 1830s. Heights 3½ inches (88 mm) and 2½ inches (63 mm).

pelling pencils, visiting-card cases and silver-mounted claret jugs. In the second half of the nineteenth century the company made large numbers of scent bottles and vinaigrettes, often in collaboration with manufacturers of glass and ceramics. Commemorative bottles marking Queen Victoria's Golden Jubilee in 1887, for which the Worcester Royal Porcelain Company made the bottles and Sampson Mordan the silver-plated mounts, are examples of this type of partnership. The firm made double-ended bottles, bottles in the form of opera glasses, bottles

LEFT: *One of a pair of Apsley Pellatt scent bottles in the Victoria and Albert Museum. This bottle has an intaglio portrait of Queen Adelaide, and its companion a portrait of William IV. 1831-7. Height 4⅛ inches (105 mm).*
RIGHT: *Cylindrical cut-glass bottle in a crown-shaped holder. English or Irish, mid nineteenth century. Height 5 inches (127 mm).*

A selection of Mordan bottles. The cut-glass bottle in the shape of a fish was made in collaboration with Thomas Webb and Sons, who registered the design in 1884. In the foreground is a bottle made from a real sea shell. About 1870-1900.

incorporating pillboxes and many other ingenious designs. Mordan bottles are often marked. If the mount is silver the maker's mark SM is stamped alongside the hallmark. Mounts in other metals have the inscriptions S MORDAN & Co, MAKERS engraved around the edge, or under the lid of smelling-salt bottles one sometimes finds the mark of a crown with S MORDAN & Co, LONDON under a glass slip.

From 1842 it was possible for a manu-facturer to register a new design which he wished to protect from imitations. An article included in the Registry of Designs was protected for three years against plagiarism by a rival manufacturer. The manufactured article would be marked with a diamond-shaped device or, from 1883, with a Registration Number (Rd No). The original drawings and a descrip-tion of each article are now kept at the Public Record Office at Kew. The 1880s seem to have been the period when the

Two bottles made to com-memorate Queen Victor-ia's Golden Jubilee in 1887. The bottles are by the Royal Worcester Porcelain Company while the silver-plated mounts are by Sampson Mordan, who registered the designs in 1886. Heights 3½ inches (88 mm) and 2¼ inches (56 mm).

greatest number of designs for scent bottles was registered; they were mostly in the form of novelties. Scent bottles were made in the shape of lifebelts, willow-patterned plates, nuts and birds' eggs.

A most striking scent-bottle design was registered by Thomas Webb and Sons of

ABOVE: *Novelty scent bottles in a variety of forms including a dagger, a Doulton stoneware book, a realistic glass lemon and a curious silver-gilt bottle in the form of a gold nugget. Mid nineteenth century to early twentieth century.*

RIGHT: *These bottles are all ceramic. The egg bottles were made by James Macintyre and Company of Burslem in a variety of sizes and colourings. If it was not for the registration number printed on each bottle they could almost be mistaken for real eggs.*

A group of scent bottles in silver and semi-precious stones in a style which was also fashionable for jewellery in the 1860s and 1870s. Several of these bottles have Birmingham hallmarks dating from 1869 to 1875. Average height 2 inches (50 mm).

Stourbridge in 1884. It was a bottle in the shape of a bird's head and was made in cameo glass. This technique, lost since Roman times, was rediscovered after many years of experimentation by John Northwood in the 1870s. By the 1880s cameo glass was being manufactured in

Stourbridge on a commercial scale. The large and elaborate pieces, made to special commission and shown at exhibitions, were time-consuming and extremely expensive to produce, but in the scent bottle manufacturers had a small, simply shaped object which could be made

Cameo-glass scent bottles including the bird's-head bottle registered by Thomas Webb and Sons in 1884. This example is in blue glass with white overlay but the design was made in a number of colours. Length of large bottle 9¼ inches (235 mm).

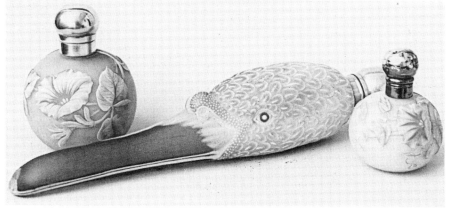

25

relatively quickly and cheaply.

Cameo glass is made of opaque coloured glass cased with an opaque white layer. The decoration is formed by removing the unwanted areas of the upper layer, leaving the design in relief against the coloured background. In the early days of making cameo glass this was done by grinding away unwanted glass on a wheel, but this was soon replaced by the quicker method of acid etching. Even though this eliminated a certain amount of labour, cameo glass still required a good deal of hand finishing. It is the fine quality of the hand finishing of the surface detail which gives cameo glass its attractive shaded effects. The feathers on the Thomas Webb and Sons bird's-head bottle are each individually hand-finished. This was an unusual subject for decoration as most scent bottles are decorated with flower designs. Cameo-glass bottles are usually of a squat globular shape or the tapering tear shape which was popular in the late nineteenth century. Some short cylindrical bottles are also to be found, but these are often of an inferior quality.

Cameo glass in a very different style was made by the French glassmaker Émile Gallé, who worked in the art nouveau style and whose work was greatly influenced both by his interest in botany and by his admiration of the Chinese glass of the eighteenth century. He experimented with different effects in opaque and semi-translucent coloured glass. His work has a fluid quality which is absent in the rather stiff design of English cameo glass.

At the end of the nineteenth century and in the early part of the twentieth, very elaborate travelling cases were made by Sampson Mordan, Mappin and Webb and others. These might contain velvet-lined jewellery compartments, manicure instruments, blotters and pockets for writing paper as well as an array of bottles and jars for cosmetics. Contemporary advertisements show that these greatly elaborated descendants of the eighteenth-century *nécessaire* could cost over £60.

Although this bottle by Gallé is made by a technique similar to English cameo glass the effect is totally different. The shape of this bottle is reminiscent of Chinese snuff bottles. About 1900. Height 4¼ inches (108 mm).

26

RIGHT: *Green glass scent bottle in pierced silver case decorated with a carnation design in the art nouveau style. The case has the London hallmark for 1903. Height 6¾ inches (170 mm).*

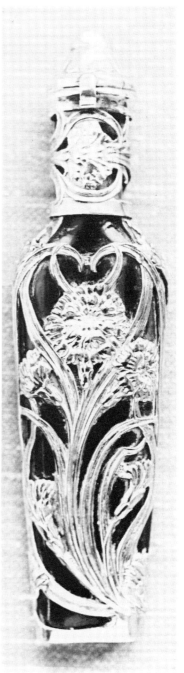

BELOW: *Massive spherical cut-glass bottle with embossed silver-hinged mounts over a ground-glass stopper. London hallmark for 1897. Height 5 inches (125 mm).*

Commercial scent bottles for D'Orsay's 'Le Lys' and Forvil's 'Cinq Fleurs' made by Lalique in the 1930s.

THE TWENTIETH CENTURY

In 1907 Francois Coty invited René Lalique to design, firstly, labels for scent bottles and, shortly after, new forms for the bottles themselves, which would complement the fragrance they contained. Lalique had turned to glassmaking late in his career, having established his reputation as one of the foremost French jewellers working in the art nouveau style. Many of his bottles continued in the art nouveau style, being decorated with nude or classically draped dancing female figures (Isadora Duncan was at the height of her fame at the time). Others incorporated classical motifs, including Pan masks, while from the late 1920s art deco designs predominate. Lalique made bottles for many perfumers, such as Guerlain, Houbigant, D'Orsay, Roger et Gallet and Worth, and including the famous star-studded globular bottle for *Je Reviens*.

As well as commercial bottles Lalique also made non-commercial bottles, often as part of *garnitures de toilette* or dressing-table sets which also included jars for creams and powders and pin bowls.

Lalique's bottles were mass-produced but nevertheless express the luxurious qualities of the perfumes at a time when the market for cosmetics was expanding as never before. The bottles were moulded in demi-crystal, which required little finishing when it came out of the mould. Many have a frosted appearance, achieved by acid etching, sometimes in combination with polished areas. Success inevitably brought a rash of imitations, both by other French glassmakers and also from Czechoslovakia.

René Lalique died in 1945. The present-day company of Cristal Lalique continues to make bottles for prestigious French perfumers, notably for Nina Ricci. The *L'Air du Temps* bottle with bird-shaped stopper, which was designed by Marc Lalique in the late 1940s, is probably the best known.

An important development in the marketing of perfumery occurred in 1923 when Coco Chanel introduced her famous *No. 5*. This was the first time that a couturier had entered the field, but other fashion houses were quick to realise that scent provided an opportunity to reach a far wider public than could ever afford their luxurious clothes. In the next few years the houses of Worth, Lanvin and Patou introduced their own perfumes. The fashion houses were particularly sensitive to the necessity to present the product in suitably elegant packaging, and it is with the introduction of the couturiers' influence that we finally see the end of the old practice of selling scent in utilitarian bottles to be decanted into the customer's own decorative bottle. Couturiers' scent bottles reflect the styles of the fashion houses; Chanel adopted an elegant square bottle with bevelled edges, which is used to this day, but when the inventive Elsa Schiaperelli launched her *Shocking* she presented it in an amusing bottle modelled as a shapely dressmaker's dummy (sometimes said to be based on the proportions of Mae West) with a tape-measure around the neck.

In the 1920s and 1930s there was an enormous expansion in the sales of cosmetics and perfumery. Inexpensive perfumes were often imaginatively pack-

Pair of Lalique scent bottles in moulded demi-crystal decorated with Pan masks and swags of flowers. The glass has an acid-etched surface giving it a matt appearance. Marked 'R Lalique' in etched script and moulded capitals. About 1925-32. Height 5 inches (125 mm).

aged. *Evening in Paris* was sold in dark blue bottles with gold labels and was available in special caskets in the shape of dancing slippers or a hotel bedroom door. The caskets were made in blue phenolic, a similar material to Bakelite. The art deco style had a great impact on scent-bottle design both for commercial and non-commercial bottles.

Today the design of the bottle and packaging has an important function in marketing scent. Bottle shapes become associated with a particular scent and are designed to reflect the image which the manufacturers seek to promote for the product. Some are strikingly modern, expressing a sophisticated image, while others rely on prettiness and femininity. Some companies such as Penhaligon and Laura Ashley have looked back to the nineteenth century for inspiration for their bottles. No doubt the collector of the future will find as much to interest him or her in today's scent bottles as we do in those of the past.

LEFT: *The success of Lalique's scent bottles inspired imitations, including examples such as this pale green bottle which has an acid-etched mark 'Czechoslovakia' on the base. 1925-35. Height 6¼ inches (158 mm).*
RIGHT: *Pale green scent bottle in the art deco style. The metal mount takes the form of a spider's web, with a spider and its prey picked out in marcasite. 1925-35. Height 7¼ inches (184 mm).*

At the cheaper end of the market scent was presented with some humour in the 1930s. Blue phenolic was used to make cases in the shape of an owl, a hotel bedroom door complete with shoes to be cleaned and a dancing slipper, which all contain bottles of 'Evening in Paris'.

FURTHER READING

Brunhammer, Yvonne (introduction by). *Baccarat, the Perfume Bottles*. Addor, 1986.
Bryant, G. E. *The Chelsea Porcelain Toys*. Medici Society, 1925.
Farrar, J. Howard. 'The Essence of Haute Couture – Commercial Perfume Bottles for Collectors' in *The Antique Dealer and Collector's Guide*, volume 39 number 5 (December 1985), 44-7.
Foster, Kate. *Scent Bottles*. The Connoisseur and Michael Joseph, 1966.
Jones North, Jacqueline Y. *Commercial Perfume Bottles*. Schiffer, USA, 1987.
Jones North, Jacqueline Y. *Perfume, Cologne and Scent Bottles*. Schiffer, USA, 1986.
Kennett, Francis. *History of Perfume*. Harrap, 1975.
Klein, Dan, and Lloyd, Ward. *The History of Glass*. Orbis, 1984.
Launert, Edmund. *Scent and Scent Bottles*. Barrie & Jenkins, 1974.
Lefkowith, Christine Mayer. *The Art of Perfume: Discovering and Collecting Scent Bottles*. Thames & Hudson, 1998.
Marsh, Madeleine. *Miller's Perfume Bottles: A Collector's Guide*. Miller's Publications, 1999.
Matthews, Leslie G. *The Antiques of Perfume*. G. Bell & Sons, 1973.
Percy, Christopher Vane. *The Glass of Lalique – A Collectors' Guide*. Studio Vista, 1977.
Sloan, Jean. *Perfume and Scent Bottle Collecting with Prices*. Wallace Homestead Book Company, 1986.
Utt, Mary Lou. *Lalique Scent Bottles*. Thames & Hudson, 1991.

UK Perfume Bottle Collectors Club publishes a quarterly newsletter. Details from Linda Byrne, UK Perfume Bottle Collectors Club, PO Box 1936, Bath BA1 3SD.

PLACES TO VISIT

Many museums have scent bottles, but they are usually part of collections of ceramics, glass or costume accessories. Before making a special journey make sure that what you want to see will be on show. It is essential to make a prior arrangement with the curator if you want to see material which is in store.

Cheltenham Art Gallery and Museum, Clarence Street, Cheltenham, Gloucestershire GL50 3JT. Telephone: 01242 237431. <www.cheltenham.gov.uk/agm> (About sixty scent bottles, not always on display, including one by Apsley Pellatt.)

Harris Museum and Art Gallery, Market Square, Preston, Lancashire PR1 2PP. Telephone: 01772 258248. <www.preston.gov.uk> (A collection of over 2700 scent bottles, mostly nineteenth-century.)

National Museum of Ireland, Kildare Street, Dublin 2. Telephone: (0353) 1677 7444. (Examples of late eighteenth- and nineteenth-century Irish glass bottles.)

Victoria and Albert Museum, Cromwell Road, South Kensington, London SW7 2RL. Telephone: 0171 938 8500. <www.vam.ac.uk> (Scent bottles include eighteenth-century enamel, porcelain and glass examples.)

The Ruth Warner Collection, Ashford, Kent. Telephone: 01233 636185. A private collection of scent bottles, mostly nineteenth- and twentieth-century commercial bottles. Can be seen by appointment only.

Wedgwood Museum, Josiah Wedgwood & Sons Ltd, Barlaston, Stoke-on-Trent, Staffordshire ST12 9ES. Telephone: 01782 204141. <www.wedgwood.com> (Jasperware bottles included in displays of the factory's wares.)

Commercial scent bottles continue to be used to promote an image for the perfume they contain. This bottle, with its whimsical stopper rather like a piece of modern sculpture, was designed by Robert Granai for Guerlain's 'Parure' in the mid 1970s.